Poetic Medicine

By

Shu-Wonna Gregory Young

authorHOUSE™

1663 LIBERTY DRIVE, SUITE 200
BLOOMINGTON, INDIANA 47403
(800) 839-8640
WWW.AUTHORHOUSE.COM

First published by AuthorHouse 03/04/05

ISBN: 1-4208-2409-0 (sc)
ISBN: 1-4208-3960-8 (e)

Printed in the United States of America
Bloomington, Indiana

This book is printed on acid-free paper.

Table of Contents

Writers Block

So many ideas and thoughts just don't know where to begin
So many emotional feelings that are held within
Do you write on fiction or nonfiction
Or things you've hoped for prayed for or even wishing
Mind is blank but yet filled with so much good information
Imagination soars with pleasant sayings and ways that you loose
total concentration
Your eyes wander back and forth from your pen to your clock
You've just received a writers first page of writers block

The Reader

Take a moment to step foot into a journey of emotions
With laughs and cries thoughtful expressions and knowledgeable
thoughts
Take these words and create a positive path one that you can only
find in a comforting expression

Blazed

Blazed is what I feel when you kiss me
Not softly, but roughly.

Blazed is what I get when you're holding me and don't want to let
go.

Blazed is what I get when you stare at me with your sexy eyes,
knowing we can't get intimate.

Blazed is what I feel when my body's ready to give in and do what
comes natural with you.

Blazed is the feeling I have when you run your finger across my
neck.

Blazed is what I get when I think about you and I alone in our own
home.

Many people get blazed up with anger, but I, I blaze up with
passion because your words touches and inner most expressions
sets my whole body on fire.

Two Diamonds

I was told you were special and unique in your own way.

I was told you were a shining gem with a glare that lights up a room.

I was told that what you've found in me is rare and priceless.

Just like the perfect set of diamonds, it took time for you and I to find each other.

Just like diamonds we have a distinguished look about ourselves.

Just like diamonds we are pure, clean, and imperfectly flawless.

We are two diamonds that have a celestial glow.

And let's not let our shines fade away but always keep a glare that makes us both happy.

Small Potatoes

Life is full of small potatoes it is the minor and insignificant things
It is the things we think are minute and insignificant in life
They can be things that make us ponder
They can be things that make us creative
A combination of everything in life
It seems though that life's small things makes great and successful
things

Just as the small potatoes can help nourish a starved man
So is it the small potatoes of life
This can bring bountiful blessings.

The Prayer

Pray to the Lord to help me in every situation, help me in my time
of need and vexations
Pray to the Lord that heritages of all get along with each other
Keeping in mind his saying to love one another
Pray to the Lord to be bountiful with his blessings and that I may
not return to my evil ways but learn from those bad lessons
Pray to the Lord that hunger in the world comes to a halt and that
the fighting of the nations have no more revolts
Lord helps us all everyday in each way, help those who don't come
to you to see that they must pray

Friendships

Friendships are built on trust and honesty
Friendships are the gathering of happiness and serenity
Even though at times looking for a friend of that fashion can be
hard
Some you keep some slip away and there are even some you
eventually have to guard
Friendships can bring the best and worst out in someone especially
when they are true
Friendships can last forever when they have a solid foundation
Friendships that are like this are part of Gods wonderful creations

Hear Me

I've drifted from you. I've closed out on you. I thought I was happy when you made me sad.

You asked what I wanted out of you. I said right, right is all I want. You set back and laughed.

Did you really care did you truly understand me?

Did you take time to just understand the facts of a matter, but also principle listen to me intensely because my voice could become silence from your presence at anytime

Moments of Salem

Every now and then we all get our moments of love, humor, life, fame.

Salem better known as Zion which means peace, all the writing expressions are my moments of peace.

Just for a moment reality, fantasy, along with feeling brings me my moment of peace.

My moments of Salem.

Defining a Good Man

A good man is essential in a woman's life. He must have character, charm and a sense of humor.

What makes a good man? a man that is independent, but knows when to ask for help. This is a good man.

A man that treats a girl, a young lady and a woman just like he would in respect to his mother or sister is a good man.

A man that can stand his own ground and speak up when faced with trials but yet can keep quiet when needed is a good man.

A man that's willing to teach, yet eager to learn is a good man.

A man that's not afraid to show emotion is a good man.

Men that can make love in the worse way but makes it feel like a gentle May breeze is a good man.

A man that takes home training serious enough from childhood to adulthood is a good man.

A man that is willing to commit himself to God, relationships and work is a good man.

A man that takes care of his own is a good man.

A man that has patience, consistency, yet lack pride is a good man.

Are you my man?

Further more, are you a good man?

Expressions of Endearment

Everything about you truly means something to me.

When you look at me your eyes tell me you are focused and real.

The touch of your hands makes me feel secure as if I know you will always be there to rely upon.

Your hugs are like pillars with strong beams that make me feel wanted.

Your kisses are soft and gentle, that lets me know you have feelings and with each kiss is an expression or message of endearment which makes me want to kiss you forever.

Your words are comforting, knowing you can communicate in a mild spirit. And your smile is part of light to a great path in my life that's filled with sweet sounds, pleasures, desires, fantasies, and surprises.

I love you truly from my creative heart. I long for the day when I am able to express my expressions of endearment thoroughly to you.

I Thought

I thought love and life would be different.
The thought on love was that when two people met,
They were honest and truly showed much love to one another.
I found out that most of what love was based on for me was lies.
I thought life would be somewhat testing but in the end all
questions would be answered to it.
I found out life has its ups and downs and that if it's going to
smoothly,
Something must be wrong.
The things in life and love I thought
Should be of extra mundane concerns but also when I thought
the people around me and the person I care for took my thoughts
serious.

One

When I think of one I think of us.

I think of unity.
I think of harmony.
I think of complete rest.

When I think of one I think of the meaning of the one rose that I
extend to you for being there for me when times seem dark.
When I think of one I think of the peace that you and I can enjoy
as long as we have God in our relationship.
I think of one when we kiss, for we are both feeling an expression
of endearment that makes our hearts grow stronger together.
When I think of one I think of the friendship, relationship,
teamwork and effort that you and I put into us.

Realize

I realize that you are still in thought, for some reason I can't shake the feeling.

I realize that you were not ready to completely love, but fear that when you are ready who will it be?

I realize what I found in you was a brother, a friend, a soul mate, but I found out you wanted to be just in my history.

I realize that this is life, not a book or a movie, yet I hope one day my page or scene will be brighter and even better.

I realize that I may never hold your hand, embrace, kiss, communicate or even laugh with you in my old age, but I do hold on to good memories.

I realized that it's true you don't always get what you want, but it hurts even more when you realize one day that I was truly in love with you.

Questions

When you look at me, what do you see?

When you touch me what do you feel?

When you are communicating with me, what do you hear?

When you kiss me, what do you taste?

When I tell you I love you, what part of that do you grasp?

When I caress your face, how does your blood run?

And when I ask questions, what do you think about me?

The Additive

In my great receipt of life I was missing something.
Something essential that would persevere me alive, help me keep
my love for people my patience and my kindness.

I found an additive that had a little love, peace, kindness, passion,
sexuality, vigor, eagerness, patience and warmth all in the same one
bottle.

And I opened it, it had a sweet smelling odor that drove me wild.

Thank you for being the additive in my life. You've added so much
to it and preserved me for life with so much meaning.

Are you my boy companion?

Are you conspicuous, is your head refined like gold, is your hair like that of the raven are your eyes like that of a dove very focused?

Are your cheeks like a garden bed of spice and are your lips a smooth as an ancient wine.

Are your hands like strong gold towers? Your abdomen, is it like an ivory plate? Are your legs as strong and sturdy as marble?
Is your palate sweet and does just looking at you makes me say everything about you is desirable?

Blessed

To be fortunate takes patience, persistence, and prayer, and it also means chances.

Patience is what was and still is part of our blessings. We value what we have now and look forward to the future.

Persistence is shown through a day to day act of communication, which in turn shows love, that everyday makes our foundation solid, it is also there, when we feed off of each others attention.

Prayer has always been essential. Our heavenly father knew what we each needed, wanted yearned, for and desired by communicating with him, he helped us find each other. And with each prayer we began to become more specific and persistent and with that we relied upon God to give us more patience.

The chance came when we meet and seen the hard work that patience, persistence, and prayer brought us and with these implement.

I not only consider it an honor to be yours but truly a blessing.

Ghetto Love Letter

You sit and talk all this yang, and ain't up to know good

You've lied to me, you've cheated on me, and still keep feeding me bull

You need to get off your lazy ass, and get a real life

Get a job, get a car, make some money lie in your pocket before you call me your wife

Maybe if you get some friends you can keep yourself occupied

Stop setting in front of the TV letting the time fly by

I love you baby, but I have it up to here with your shit

Excuse me,
No you didn't just call me a "bitch"

You know I'm tired of you treating me like a hook on the street

If you look real hard, you'll see that I am truly a lady
Treat me with R-E-S-P-E-C-T
And I will give you that back

Ghetto love, I do love you just because we live in a situation where things just aren't just so perfect we tend to forget who we really are at heart

My ghetto love I love you with you I don't want to live without

I Want To Make Love

I want to make love,
Love to you.

To make love.
What is it to me?

To make love is to share you.
Your life, your thoughts, your ideas, your pain and sorry
Your joy and laughter.

To make love is the put the person in your life next to your creator.
To make love is tell another passerby that you are all ready in love.
To make love is to show respect and be respected.

To make love is to hold your love close at night, to touch in a soft
and passionate manner.
To make love is a lot of things mainly to a make a commitment.
Are you ready to make love?

I am.
I want to make love.

To Be Enslaved

To be held in contempt. To be put to a halt
Upon determination, dreams and that of mere reality.
To sweat when you don't have to. To cry when you don't want to
feel pain when you shouldn't have to. To have no love shown to
you when needed.
To be put down and belittled.
To be enslaved.

Death

Hey it's me you know the person you dread to come to your door
The one who your whole life you've tried to stay away from
I'm sorry for the pain and sorrow that I bring
I thought I'd be bringing some serenity
From all the aches and pains you felt
The ones you didn't feel as you slept
So I took it upon myself to put you in an everlasting sleep
Well, that is it depends upon your faith in the lord
Now that you know my reason for coming, please forgive me do
not fret, yes my name is death I know you shall not forget

Giving

They say if a person throws off love, love is what they shall gain in return
In some cases this is true and others it is not.

I've found in you not only a blessing but a river quenching my thirst that has overflowed with love

I've gave you my time you've given me yours. I gave you my energy, you've given me yours.
I've gave you my acts of patience you've given me yours.
I've gave you my heart and you've given me yours.

I've put my all into us and you've done the same.
I'm willing to give up my last name and you're wiling to give me yours.

I can say I have thrown off love and you have returned the same to me. It's all about giving and willingness. Now I have bountiful blessings that I want to impart to you, you've shared yours let me share mine.

Defining a Good Woman

A good woman must be having seriousness, humor, and character.

A good woman is a woman who speaks her mind and stands her ground. She is educated and independent, yet knows she needs help from a good man.

A good woman respects her man and those within her communicating circle. She carries herself so that she's not disrespected but respected.

She loves her man in a way where he's focused on only her. She's not a jealous prideful or conceited type. She puts God first in her life and she's not a follower of man, but a leader.

A good woman believes in herself and her dreams. She also accomplishes them.
A good woman has rare qualities. Am I that woman? Are you that woman?

His Song

He took my hand and led me to a far away place.

He sang me a love song that made my heart race.

He told me it was his song that he sang just for me.

The way he felt, the love he showed he sang on one knee.

He looked in my eyes as he sang this lonely song.

As our eyes would meet his words would get very strong.

His song he sang to me will always remain in my head.

For I sing the song now everytime I rest my head.

Hopefully it won't be long, that he and I can together sing his lonely song.

Inside of Me

Inside of me lies anger, pain, and a broken heart.
A heart that was built up with high hopes of love.

Inside of me is frustration and an eagerness that races hoping
things will change for the better.

Inside of me are parts of a commitment that I hold dear, that I may
never let go of. Not being able to speak, touch, or hold you build
rage in me.

So I pray to God to give me strength and a calm spirit so that I can
deal with all the twisted emotions
Inside of me.

Before You Go

Before you go let me tell you how much you mean to me.

Before you go let me tell you what you do to me, give me the chance to let you know I need you here with me.

Let me tell you I need love if I don't have it I am unhappy. Before you go let me tell you I love you, let me kiss you one more night one more day for eternity.

Before you go let me love you cherish you take care of you and share myself, my goals and my life before you go.

A Reflection of Fear

I fear the pain of yesterday today. The pains of yesterday brought harsh words, mean thoughts, betrayal, adulterated actions, blisters of flesh no concerns, no cares, no fears, no friends, no warm love.

I fear the pain of yesterday today, even though it was not it was not my actually pain. I've seen it heard and sometimes felt it through the cries of what was mine.

Now I'm faced with the challenge in life and I have a reflection of fear from yesterday today

Guidance

I was a lost soul that needed direction and you provided a map that gives me meaning, comfort, examples and the direction in life that I needed.

I found it easier to walk in this path it was straight and had no faults.

This guidance I am able to share with all who will listen. It has taught me to be an individual and also a follower of right.

With this guidance I know that anything is possible and that it will lead me into eternal happiness.

My Path

Dear Lord,

My path in life seems long, it also seems hard. You told me lord to exert myself vigorously. You also said do not tire out and that my deliverance is near, this I truly believe.

But for now my life has moveable seas in my path of life. I've experienced the ups and downs of heartache the currents and wind drifts of sadness. In my path I've tried not to get sidetracked by the things of the world even though there have been a lot of obstacles along the way. Despite them, I've tried to stay focused and because I've concentrated you promised that I would be blessed.

And every now and then I experience those blessings which are truly grand.

Dear Lord, blessed is the womb in which I was carried and the man that put me there for they have raised me so that eternal life is my aim and goal in my path.

Ooh Girl

Ooh girl I truly understand he did what you said, "Girl what's wrong with that man?"

Ooh girl I know that outfit you got is fly.

Ooh girl my head itch, I think my scalp is dry.

Ooh girl do I look like I'm putting on a few pounds or two.

Ooh girl you're going where to eat, girl I want to go with you

Ooh girl that girl said she was a gold digger ain't it a shame she's a true born nigga

Ooh girl my little friend came and visited me this week I'm kind of cranky and moody and I think I need to go to sleep.

Ooh girl you are my true ace boon coon

Ooh girl what will I do without you

Pimpernel Concerns

I hope and pray that you or your love is not like that of a pimpernel.

Closing up yourself when our somewhat illusive weather is bad.

When all I can see is one-sided emotions.

Open yourself to me through tribulations, pains and when there's unpleasing and repulsive views made or seen.

Show your pimpernel concerns through all season of good and bad.

Return It

A wise and yet close friend said, "Men and women are just alike,"

If this is the case return the good toward each other. When on tries you try harder. When one gives you give more. When one shares all you give all you got. When one tells you that you're in thought. Take a moment and see their good. Whatever you see or hear in good return it, it's life's circle of love.

Just Notice

Though I may not be able to solve your problem.
I'm here to lend a helping hand though I can't correct your wrong
I'm here to try and understand though I won't partake in your ways
of evil deceit.
I will if you're willing to change help you get on your feet.

Though I'll smile and nod I won't be your worst critic, however I'll
try to show you your wrong by being optimistic though sometime
you make me feel you don't put stock in some of my words.
At least give me the acknowledgement that I have been heard.

Friend or Enemy

To love is an action all of us should have

Whether it is loving another human being or love of selfish desires.

To attain and achieve we must love.

To gain and succeed, we must love.

To persecute and kill we must love.

Love is an act that based on individual can be a pleasant and warm thing or it can be a fable of emotions.

It can be patient if you choose for it to be it can suffer long if let it be.

It can be mistaken for its evil twin of infatuation.

That's what Knees Are For

When days are long and you seem overly stressed and kindness
and patience are put to the test remember that's what knees are
for. When you want to be heard among the crowd and stand up
for what you know but your resistant is bearing and persecution has
gotten you on all time low, remember that's what knees are for.
When it seems no one around understands your problem but
somehow they want to give you all the advices on how to solve
them remember that's what knees are for.
When you concord good with evil, and your day seems to be
going smooth with no upheaval remember that's what knees are
for. Good or bad he has opened up his ear he also lent you a
hand so that you'd realize he was near for he asks us to talk to him
throughout our day simplicity yet nothing more. He won't make us
do it or push us to the floor. If you find yourself not talking to him
regularly ask him to help you because remember that's what knees
are for.

Extending Attention

I've got my eye on you, this I believe you know by attention I've extended to you.

I extend attention to you through letters, cards, calls, gifts, hugs and kisses.

Make sure you know that I am for real and there is no schemes that come along with me and my love.

Nothing extravagant just simple things like God, he gives us attention through creation and how thankful we are.

Question, are you thankful for the attention extended to you?

There is more happiness in giving say the Lord. I am truly happy extending attention to you and feel blessed.

What about you, how do you feel about extending attention to me?

Keep the Fire Burning

Symbolically speaking I am a fire full of warmth and blazing with much passion. You are a sturdy log that keeps me burning.

Do you realize if you don't keep me burning, or inflamed with passion I'll die out?

Throw into me your logs of hugs, kisses, touches, and embraces and I will show you as time pass, how warm I can keep you.

My job and purpose is to satisfy you and keep you comfortable. I can do this to the utmost gratification of your desires.

I can only put out what sturdy logs you put into me, for now smaller logs are fine, but bigger logs burns longer.

Can you as time pass keep this fire burning?

Doors

People are like doors in so many ways.
We are open for anything. Our minds, our hearts, our lives.
Willing to let a stranger enter and take chances.

Some of us never open or swing. We are firm, locked, and
independent. Making sure we secure what's ours.

Like doors are we shaped and molded into fine grain and hinges
that are strong. Do we hold locked inside of us sturdiness of mind
and a protected heart or are we full of opportunity.

Faith

Faith is an expectation of hope it is what make us have a passion for our dreams of success. It is what makes a friendship, swing on the edge, excitement.

It is what makes a spouse continue wearing a ring once that love is long gone.
It is what makes a teacher see the heart's eye of a student.
It is what makes optimism in ones attitude that things will work out.
It is what makes one a strong person.
It is something seen by its beholder that is good to the soul rather big or small it's a motivator of a wise one's life.

Words

You were told that you were beautiful and that your eyes were as bright as the sun.

Your smile was like the opening of a flower after the morning dew. You were told that your skin was as soft as the cotton in the filed of your heritage.

And that your voice though mellow, was of great wisdom and guidance backed by strength.

You were told all those things by a person who said they wanted and needed you in their life.

Why then did you feel like you were ugly your eyes only seen grim and darkness, you were unhappy like a child without nourishment or love from its mother.

You felt like the thorns and splinters of your heritage and your voice was always unheard.

Reality has come to the fold about actions speaks louder than words and how beautiful words are not always truthful.

Laughter

Laughter is a good thing a warm emotion that being a human can bring
Laughter is shown in times of jokes, silly tales and funny images to the eye
It should be a daily thing in ones life
Laughter is something that gives of ourselves a sacrifice one of goodness and wholesome ways
One you'll have in all your days
Laughter is here today and tomorrow

Give Me My Rose

Give me my rose while I'm vibrant and full of vigor
While the sun still shines on my face
Give me my rose while I walk the earth while my heart can still
feel happiness and disgrace
Give me my rose when you see me standing tall
When achievements and success is in the air
Do not give me my rose when I'm laying in a box already covered
with flowers and when you words to me will be unheard and
when nothing but darkness will be upon my face because I will be
entrapped until the calling of my Savior calls me out
So today while you see me, hear me, and can touch me give me my
rose

Just Wanted You

Okay, I made a huge mistake. It seemed to me your love was delayed though I'm not trying to make an excuse just hear me out before you just refuse.

He told me wanted all of me. His style and class sparked my curiosity.

Baby it happen so sudden it was just one time one night. I knew it was wrong, but it felt so right.

See I just wanted you, I know it was ignorant, selfish and rood. But believe me sweetheart he was just a substitute.

See you have something he will never attain. A lasting thing a bond, a union, a last name.

He had for one night my emotion and body for a moment in time. But you have all of me body, soul, and mind.

Baby it was just you I wanted and I truly apologize. Can you forgive me and love me still forever or maybe I'm pushing it. How about one day at a time
the winks and remarks of him in his saying of, "Sweetheart you're so fine." Wasn't nothing to me but chump change better yet it wasn't even worth my time.

Your time and energy, hugs and kisses, just some me time you know, a little attention.

Many nights while you were out I prayed that you'd come home and just hit me. I just wanted you to love me completely.

Caught in a moment of passion I'm sorry. I'm sorry from this day I tell you the truth, because baby all I really wanted was just you.

His Messages

Everyday he leaves me a message one that expresses his feelings his wants and desires.

He tells me what he thinks of me what he hopes we achieve what little he expects from me and what he wants from me.

His messages leave smiles upon my face for the rest of the day and at night even though he's not near I can always listen to his messages which are truly from his heart.

It Will Work Out Fine

I am patient I try to be kind everything I want in life I don't always get.

But I believe that love everything it will work out fine, whatever comes know that your heavenly father will stick with you, it will work out fine.

Have faith smaller than a mustard seed bigger than earth believe in love it will work out fine.

Even though I want to be with you I must remember what's best, love is not jealous and it's not loud, not boastful or bragging, but love believes all things and my love.

I believe it will all work out fine.

My First Love

My first love brought me joy and peace.

My first love brought me truth and honesty.

My first love brought me comfort when I was depressed and hope for my future.

My first love sculpted me into who I am and what I am.

My first love gave me a talent and a gift to share with the world.

My first love gave me life and I would like to thank him because he will always remain my first love, thank you Lord.

No More

No more will I touch your face.
No more will I feel you strong hands in mine.
No more will I hear your voice.
No more will I be able to express to you how I feel for you, for it
will be indecent.
No more will I be able to spend time to speak of serious things like
our lives, our future. Jokes for now are not even mentioned.

We conduct ourselves as mere strangers. Not having any love for
each other in us. For we both know this is a lie, but we can not live
the truth of our love no more.

Passion Rose

He sent passion roses in lovely vase.

He sent his heart to me through someone with a warm embrace.

These were six steam roses, each with its own meaning and character. Each with its own spontaneous sayings.

And a card attached which told me his feelings. Even though not much was said what was said was awe inspiring and touched my heart.

He sent me passion roses he sent me his heart. He sent his feelings hoping that we'd never part.

Poetic Medicine

We all have an antidote in life one of comfort and one of lyrical stride one that makes us think one that makes us laugh one that makes us cry everyone of us has a poetic medicine

Whether it's a soulful sound, a rhythmic rap or a historical baseline of blues take time to embrace your poetic medicine

Three Cords

I am a cord playing a lonesome tune, you are a cord that is stronger than I, but I make you sound so pleasant to the listeners' ears.

Together we can do just about anything you are the strength and I am the might.

We need powers, power for more greater then what anyone else can give, power beyond what is normal.

And who has that no one but our creator so let him be our third cord so that to the listeners we can be strong mighty and powerful.

And with his bond, no one can tear us apart, because he who is that third cord will never leave us unless we leave him. Come now let us be harmoniously united as those three *cords*.

Committed I am

You can say sweet and soulful sayings that appear appealing.

What you forgot is that with my heart I all ready have dealings.
Though at least that's what you say and even though I reject you try
to woo me day by day

Committed I am

I have no loose chains no variation of keys for key hold see I'm
into what's mine let me repeat I'm into what's or should I say who's
mine.

Committed I am to a cracked yet tainted vessel, but this vessel has
value even with flaws I'll hold it Nestled

Though I've joked to you treated you kindly and sometime even
vented, know this one thing still I am very committed.

Continue

To the man who was disrespected on the job.
For the women who are looked upon as inferior
To the child who didn't know it's father and its mother abandon
not only them but their heart
To the grandparents who never seen their grandchildren but only
gained the title.
To the husband who walked away from being betrayed.
To the wife who was told she was not loved
To the students who tried and still didn't get the passing grade
To the boyfriend who caught his girl cheating
To the girl with the nappy hair big lips big eyes and thick thighs
To the folks who don't have just a home in the streets.
To the ones who never felt like they fit in.

To the encourager who never got encouraged
To the ones who forgave but never is shown forgiveness
For those who put forth effort even small and it's not thinkable.

For every inch you somewhat show love know that you are loved.

For every tragedy there's a solution.
For every tear there's a healing
For every time you really try it becomes common

So continue trying, continue making things right, making effort.
There's always a revelation to your situation

Majestic Man

Enthusiastic cordial and humorous you set my spirit free
Majestic man you bring me joy and serenity
Strong sturdy passionate frame
When I see you it's like looking into celestial lights I just want to
say your name
I can feel you when I eat and sleep I can taste you in my dreams
It makes me feel whole and complete
Speaking with strength yet speaking with a tamed tongue
Loving me wholly unconditionally as if I was an understanding one

Majestic man you are one of a kind
Set my body on fire and spirits run free
You release everything in me
Heart, soul, and mind.

With these hands

With these hands I molded and produced you.

I gave you creativity and also appeal and ways of productivity.

With these hands I comforted you with my gentle touch, only letting you take so much.

With these hands I want you to know that I will not create evil.

For I want you to know there's a reason it's allowed listen its a test a challenge from the Devil.

With these hands I can and will immensely carry out my will.

With these hands know there's that purposes I planned for you will be fulfilled.

Reconciliation

It doesn't mean to chase
It doesn't mean single
It doesn't mean to get and not give
It doesn't mean partial agreement
It means two people, two parties
It means to unify
It means to get together to agree

Thanks for Making Love to Me

Thank you my love for making love to me.

Through your words, actions, gifts of expressions you have truly touched my inward parts without physically touching me.

Thanks for making love to me in the sense of communicating being there when I need you.

Thanks for making love in the sense of laughter I can always rely upon joyful moments with you.

Thanks for making love in the sense of caring and understanding the love you've shown and expressed feels good to me.

Thanks for making love to me.

We Need To Talk

It hurt so badly, the tears fall so far the lonely nights in bed the long drive in the car
The moments of the thoughts of us.
The love, the honor the trust
It happened and it stopped but it hurt
Don't you think we need to talk?
Moving forward blood, sweat and tears putting away everything all pride and fears.
Being more supportive, respectful and helping each other out
Help mend the home and make the eyes have a drought
Tears of pain can turn into tears of joy if we try
Instead of running out dropping everything and saying goodbye
Take me in your arms even if you feel you can't
You'd be amazed at what will advance
Instead of throwing your hands up saying you'll walk
Baby, set down, I love you we need to talk.

If I . . .

If I were to stare at you with no facial expression would you say I hated you?

If I were to turn and look the opposite way when you're speaking, would you say I don't listen?

If I were to have a streak of jealousy in me, would you say because of knowing what your heavenly fathers says about love is not jealous, that I don't love you?

If I were to let your hand go, would you say I'm not compassionate?

If I were to miss calling you, would you say I don't care about what happens to you in the run of a day?

If I didn't speak occasionally, would you say I had an attitude?

If I were someone else would you be happy, but if I am myself will you be content?

The Baritone Voice

I heard a voice call out to me.
A baritone voice.

It was deep, it was strong, it was stern, it was sexy, and it was sweet.
This voice grabbed something within me that made my heart
flutter.

This baritone voice had a face of warmth.
His smile was refreshing.
His eyes was lustful, and
His lips were desirable.

This voice had a body that was sleek and bold untainted and pure.
The baritone voice had goals and plans and inquired me that I was
in them, his goals and plans gave me a mental picture of my future
just like his voice.

It was strong, stern, deep, everlasting, sexual and sweet future.

This baritone voice I will treasure and hold under lock and key and
keep next to my heart because with it comes a man that has much
to offer in my eyes.

Will You

Will you be there when times get hard?
Will you comfort me at night when I can't sleep?

Will you hold me when I'm cold?
Will you put your arm around me when we are sitting side by side?

Will you hold my hand when we pray together?
Will you take more time out in the run of a day to see how I feel and what I think?

Will you continue to flirt when time has passed?
Will you whisper freaky, sexy, and soothing words in my ear when I least expect it?

Will you love me unconditionally?

Will you?

You May Not Have . . .

You may not have diamonds, gold, or silver.

You may not have the funds of those in prominent positions.

You may not have the lavish cars.

You may not have the elegant home.

You may not have a surplus of time in the run of a day.

You may not be as smart as the educated scholar.

You may not have the power to change your past.

You may not have a lifetime, but you do have a treasure in your heart that's worth more than diamonds, gold, or silver.

You do have the riches surpass and more, because you're heavenly father owns it all.

You do have mobility whether it on wheels or feet. You do have a prospect of not only having a house, but with love, peace, and understand you will have a home.

You do have the time to make sure of the more important things in life which truly are responsibilities.

You do have the smart of simplification and understanding.

You do have the power to achieve a blessed future.

You do have the knowledge to attain a lifetime.

You may not have much but you do have your heavenly father, your family, and I, And with these three elements, you lack nothing.

They Say

They said we weren't a match but, we found out we had the same background and a lot in common.

They said it wouldn't work out, but I guess they were right, but didn't know the reason why.

They said, "That I wasn't approved" by them, but who makes that decision, who am I for them or you?

They said I had talent and skill, but on the other hand I wasn't good enough.

They said there was lack of honesty but proof of the truth was before you. It was by choice rather or not you wanted to know it.

They have much to say rather it is a concern or pure nosiness, but the fact of the matter is we are individuals we make our own decision. We must live our own lives of mistakes and imperfections when they are not even around.

The Ecstasy of Me

The ecstasy of me
I have honey dripping from my lips like that of a honeycomb.
My words are sweet and they calm your heart and soul, smoother
than oil.

The ecstasy of me
Will make you always drink from your own cistern, my waters are
blessed.

The ecstasy of me
Will make you constantly intoxicated with my love from the hairs
on my head, to the heels of my feet.

The ecstasy of me
Has shown you that you find expression of endearment from my
kisses, wanting desires for my skin as you smell the fragrance of
love from my inward parts.

Yearn for me as if I was a sweet peach given to a starved man.
The ecstasy of me
Made you realize . . . that my eyes can read you like a book.
My stature is firm and tight as that of a vibrant virgin.
My legs and thighs are as strong as two stubborn bulls.
My breasts are as tender as the feeling of a new life that has
entered the world.
My tongue flows with milk and honey in other words.
Nice and kind things come from me, but what I have to say is also
nourishing.
The ecstasy of me is a lot of things and a lot of feelings that I know
and believe that you hold dear and in the same light I know there
is an ecstasy of you

The One

I want to be the one,
Who always catches your eye in a crowded room.

I want to be the one
That can communicate with you through the glance of our eyes.

I want to be the one
Whose voice you hear in your ear at night.

I want to be the one
By your side serving the lord.

I want to be the one
Who shares in your pain, sorrow, happy and joyous occasions.

I want to be the one,
Who accepts your imperfections
I want to be the one,
Who takes care of you when you're ill

I want to be the one,
Who gets in heated discussions and later able to solve the problem
and make up.

I want to be the one,
Who meets you at the end of the aisle

I want to be the one,
That spends the rest of my life with you.

Eric's Inspiration

You inspired me to take chances.
You inspired me to love again.
You inspired me to dream and fantasize.
You inspired me to be more patient and calm.
You inspired me to want to care more.
You inspired me to take things I feel and express them verbally.
You inspired me to take what was in my heart and share it with others.
You inspired me to visualize my future with hope and meaning.
You inspired me more so to put my best first.
You inspired me to be overjoyed with goodness.
You inspired me more to have much faith.
Most of all,
You inspired me to truly know and realize that the love you and I share is truly from our heavenly father.
And because of your inspiration I extend gratitude because not only did and do you love me,
You inspired me to want to love you.

Kisses of Cotton

Soft and comforting is the feel of cotton and so are your kisses.

Relaxing and warm is the feel of cotton and so are your kisses.

Soothing and pure are attributes of cotton and so are your kisses.

Just like the precious time, warm heart and love that grandma put into all her quilts you put into your kisses.

Your kisses put lust, warmth, and passion throughout my body.

My love you have kisses of cotton.

To Commit

To place as a trust, to pledge have I truly committed myself to you?

I am dedicated to you and only you in this relationship.

Joy and happiness derives from within when I speak only your name.

Whenever I'm in motion with passerby the thoughts of other men aren't there.

Whenever horns honk, whistles are given and flirtatious remarks are made, I think to myself I can receive them from my man.

A wall is what I portray when it comes to other men. I share your name with them when they stop to speak.

Committed to you is a way of life, a task I gladly hold. I pledge to you unconditional love and hard work of attaining happiness.

I have showed you who I am what I am where I'm going and how I will achieve and uphold this commitment.

Hopefully you are as committed as I and together no one can break our trust our pledge or our love.

The Prince of My Heart

The prince of my heart is extraordinary he's talented, mild tempered, meek, humble, sexual and full of loving kindness.

The prince of my heart is strong, tolerant, patient, and careful.

The prince of my heart puts reality in my mind and makes my inner most thoughts weak.

I am truly grateful to be your only subject in your special kingdom.

Thank you for being the prince of my heart.

Passion

Passion is what you ask from me. Do you truly know what you're asking for?

When you ask for passion from me you're asking for an overdrive of emotions that words can't but actions can express.

When you ask for passion you're asking for repetitious and uncontrolled orgasms that never end and gets better as minutes pass.

When you ask for passion you ask for rhythmic coitus that is steady, gentle, and slow.

When you ask for passion you're asking for heat and sweat that are made with intertwined bodies.

When you ask for passion you're asking for pleasurable sounds such as moans of pleasure, whimpers of pain, and screams of gratification.

Passion is it truly what you want?

Most importantly is this what you ask from me?

May I Nourish You?

May I complement you by nourishment?

Can I not only gain from you the feeling of security but also the joy and success that lie ahead?

Even though your heavenly father tells you as a man to provide for his woman.

May I nourish you in giving back provisions in life?

Can I nourish you emotionally, mentally, physically, sexually, and spiritually?

May I nourish you in these ways so you can give me back nourishment that's based on love from all aspects?

May I nourish you in the attainable goals in life?

May I have the chance to show you how to nourish me in life, understanding and in love?

To Please My Man

To please my man, God gave me a set of seductive eyes that when captured in a stare makes my man smile.

To please my man God gave me a smile that lets him know I have trust, faith, and that I care for and will always be there.

To please my man God gave me strong but soft hands to let him know I'm willing to work to obtain our dreams yet I'm sensitive to his needs.

To please my man God gave me lips to speak with my man and let him know how I feel and to show expression of love.

To please my man, God gave me arms to embrace him in triumph and also trials.

To please my man God gave me breast that only he will be intoxicated with and have the knowledge of stimulating me.

To please my man God gave me a waist for my man to grasp, hold or thrust into whenever he needed me near.

To please my man God gave me thighs and legs to wrap around my man so that only he and I can become one.

To please my man, God gave me a firm hind that only man has right to touch when caught up in a moment of passion.

To please my man, God gave me a character, style and a rare personality that he felt my man would like.

God gave me all these things to please my man so I will give my man all of me and who I am because I want to please him.

Thinking of You

In the run of the day when I drift away in memory I think of you.

When I see couples walking hand in hand I think of you.

When I listen to love songs I think of you.

I think of the good times we had, which were many for they outweighed the bad.

I wonder how my life could be, should be and how it might be, when I think of you.

Whenever I think of you a smile appears upon my face, just as the smile that was there knowing you'd appear or just call.

There are days when I just want to say hello or see how you are, it's because I'm thinking of you.

And the reason I think of you so much is because I know that with you I was able to show love, give love, and firmly believed that you I loved.

Accomplishing Longevity

Can you and I accomplish longevity?

It is attainable, together longevity is in all aspect of our lives.

Spiritual longevity being able to let God forever be our guide in whatever we do.

Mental longevity being capable to think things through.

Emotional longevity able to console, love and care for each other.

Sexual longevity being able to keep the lust, passion, and escalated orgasms from the depth of the earth to the heights of the heavens.

Accomplish longevity in the four aspects makes it easy to maintain physical longevity.

For me being with you for eternity is my accomplishment of longevity.

Strength of a Man

The strength of a man is not just the physical make up but it in tells his mental strength and spiritual strength.

Without mental and spiritual strength one is incomplete.

To concur and succeed a man need his lifeline's his building blocks of life mentally to keep a plan, a blueprint of life. Spiritually to let the Almighty guide him in everything he does which makes a man physical appearance one of great stature and great strength.

Pay Attention Young Man

Hey young man did you notice her eyes, her lips, or maybe her thighs.

Did her attractiveness or wisdom catch your eye?

Did the stories make you sit on the edge of your set when you see her did you realize your heart skipped a beat.

Pay attention young man she's not doing this for you it is in her nature, she values her worth do you?

Pay attention young man
Do you see her work her sweat her tears, not really because there are things she keeps within and all the while with her head up high and a smile.

Can you see your diamond shine or is it faded and blurred that you can't notice.
Pay attention young man for what you saw at first if you're not focused will be seen by your enemy or a silent theft.

Focus and study her make her your curriculum of the day.

Young man please pay attention for she all ready knows she can shine without you. It was proven before you,
Can you hear her, young man Can you see her young man

This is not just your lover this is your mother, sister
maybe best friend. She's known for not being a busy body, so she's paying attention she watches your move
Young man are you paying attention

Perfect Man

The perfect man having the sounds of wisdom of the psalmist, the romantic heart of Solomon, the endurance and patience of Job, the strength of Samson the humility of David, the courage of Daniel, the self control when lead upon temptation of Joseph. The intelligence to take the lead is that of Moses and the heart of our Savior Jesus.

Yes, this is my dream this is my constant prayer, this is the man my mother and father will give my hand to. Yes, this is the perfect man.

Harmonize

Joined together we were upon a scale of music
A clef is what the Lord played in our son,
We were drawn by each others fantasia,
The strength of our vocals, are like that of platinum.
There were accidental signs in our acappella voices,
Those made our hearts grow warm and knees give out, each giving
our own cadenza
As we counter pointed ourselves in making the language of music
We made a staff a masterpiece and harmonized our love.

Through My Words

You said that I express myself through words best
Well here are my lines of between the lines, this is your test
No trifling games are played, you are my fortress my spade
Through my words there's no arguing fuss and fight
Just a chance to come correct and love each other right
I'll fight for you, but the enemy in view is bigger than me
Can't you see that I love you so I've gave it to Him You're bound to
make mistakes because you're human
Guess what you have forgotten through treatment that this is what
I am
You may say that this has made your mind disturbed
As you read, the rhythm and script if not trust in me as a person
trust me through my words

The Challenger

The challenger is one who thinks he can do it all
Beware challenger you might get challenged you might get
challenged therefore you may fall
Cunning and detestable are the ways of these ones thoughts
The implements of deception is running through the heart and
mind
The challenger is intelligent though ignorant
For his ways in every challenge is always the same
One who is competitive in every debate or game
Challenger you are afraid of what the next man can do
Challenger be careful with your challenges
For death could become of you

The Comforter and Creator

They are there to make wonders with your way of life,
They console when times are hard, they are ears when nobody else
is around,
They keep you up to date with the events in the community even if
you don't care
They anoint you head with oils of wisdom, and fade you with the
sharpest swords,
So that when you meet the world and they ask, "who made you and
instrument of beauty" you can say, "my comforter and creator",

They take out time in their lives to beautify yours, though it can
cost you a pretty penny, I guess you can't put a price on the things
that they do,
They put up with those who live in a dream world and don't want
to face reality, at times they do the impossible and they make
miracles, these are times they deserve praise,

In their domain they hold scrolls that have guidelines that you go
by, so that you know what kind of person you want to be,
They can make women look like divas and goddess form old, they
can make you go back to your heritage being the princess of Africa.

They can make men look like great actors and mighty warrior
kings.

There are some who garble at what they do and how they carry out
their ways. These are not comforter and creator these are what we
call haters.

They come from all walk of life, they are different shades of our
heavenly father.

They are the men and women who we call are barbers and
beauticians, our comforters and creators.

**Dedicated to all my favorite stylist, barbers
and beauticians**

Not a Perfect Girl

I'm not a perfect girl.

I don't have hair like that of a horse or satin fabric.

I don't have the face of a California chick or the body that society has framed as a supermodel or a walk that will make a man judge me, before knowing me but,

I do have a mind of creativity, eyes that deserve and can pierce my enemy. A heart that extends itself, hands that are diligently working, a stand about myself that shows I must be respected. I'm not a perfect girl.
The things that come with me are real and should be expected.

When I Rise

When I rise the warmth of heavenly love hits me,
Celestial lights flash into my eyes when I rise

The smell of dew makes every life giving breath worth breathing.

Like falls from islands in far lands I feel refreshed when I rise.

When I rise I think of accomplishments that I might achieve for
the day.

I think of the sun on the horizon making itself know to all men
that it will shine.

I only await the day when each rising moment is as warm,
refreshing and perfect as that of the one I get now when I rise.

Why I Live

I have a reason why I live or for that matter wake up each day.

I lives so that I can be thankful for another day in which I might don't deserve, I live so that I can see what becomes of the generation behind me, I live to experience love, compassion, lust and friendship.

I live to be a helper to someone a friend and hopefully one day a companion for life.

I live so that I can experience heartache, pain, broken heartedness, stress, depression so that I know that I am an imperfect human.

I live because this is what was intended for me to do from my heavenly father.

I live to see will I gain his most gracious prize of life.

I live to give each day my best, better than yesterday.

I live so that each day I can accomplish something I live so that each day I can learn new things.

Even though times get hard and I feel like I don't want to live I work at the things around me and reflect back on why I want to live.

To Hausoni

You were in thought today, just as you were yesterday and the day before that.

Though you feel trust is gone and broken, and hearts don't put on a show, I see that you've not tried to mend but your proving what's within.

Though you mention love is undefined in my mind, you say it is by showing.

Yet you fail to see what I am showing you at this moment for you're looking in your past.

Am I not still existing the conversations and messages of thoughts are they not effort from my part.

Are you approving me with questions you should be asking of one, have you disregarded what was in my thought and heart?

Right now at this very moment have you forgiven, to mend, to heal apology has been given but questioned if taken.

Hausoni if I'm not one to you are displaying love, out of love, show me what love is or is it complex for you. Or you say you've displayed love if you never really loved.

Unconditional what does it mean not to me but to you

In whatever you do you will always be my Hausoni unconditionally cordially continuously in love of heart and mind.

If You Love Me

If you love me,
You would treat me differently.

You would treat me as the gem that shines and makes a name for itself, for who I am and not just for what I am.

If you love me,
You would be there for me emotionally, physically, mentally and most of all,
spirituality

And not be there in sight to see but to insight me.

If you love me,
You would do what's good for us and not just you.

If you love me,
Everyone around us can see.

If you love me,
You wouldn't have to question yourself too.

If you love me,
You would put away the pain of the past.

And focus on happiness for the future.
If you loved me.

Using the Tongue Aright

Using our mouth to speak can be a very good implement. We can use it for a source of encouragement or a source of contention.

For this matter I think all can be acquiesce that the tongue can be very useful that the tongue can be very useful.

In being forgiving, our tongue can be useful, speaking out not holding a grudge which can rob us of serenity and self pride.

In reading, we are able to comprehend and interpret words so that we can use them in our speech, making ourselves shine as a high-muck-a-muck.

Using your speaking ability to the full advantage can be very soulful.

That's what the goal is in using my mouth. Question is how do you use your tongue aright?

My Love Prayer

God-

A while back you sent something heavenly into my life. A man that made me feels secure and happy. A man with realistic dreams and goals in his hands is my future. I found out he's patient and warm to be precise. I also found out that a piece of imperfection in me made him wonder.

God-

I know you do not bring anything bad upon your servants. I also know that you hate lies, but with all the honesty if I walk away from this man whose will is also to serve you, I feel I've sinned because I'd be lying and masquerading as if I didn't care for him.

God-

This feeling I'm having it's not right, it's not fair was this veneer as with the others when will love be true to me. When will it love me unconditionally?

It Is You I Miss

It is you I miss when I'm sitting in a quiet room.

It is you I miss when I'm listening to a love song.

It is you I miss when I catch sight of couples walking about hand in hand.

It is you I miss when I read that the lord tells me that love bares, hopes and believes all things and that it will endure.

It is you I miss when I turn over in the middle of the night and see nothing but pillows.

It is you I miss when the phone rings and it's someone that is not of my concern.

It is you I miss when a strange fellow ask if I got a man, and I'm able to say yes.

It is you I miss when I'm cold at night.

From this my love you can tell that I miss you a lot and I am constantly reminded of you throughout my day to day living. Just as the thought of my heavenly father and just as with him I think of you often because I love you from the depth of my soul.

Love Ransom

A captive was my heart and sore enslaved by hurtful words and sinful memories built upon lies.

You came along and made a ransom for my heart and soul, reversed the past torment with patience, love, and understanding.

You took a chance with this captive heart and soul, entrusting faith in the both, that you will not go through a fatality quite like the one you have helped correct.

The love ransom you gave I hold dear and appreciate it both heart and soul.

To Desire

To request, to wish, to hope, to long for
Is my expression of desire

To be conscious upon impulse toward something that I can
promise will be attainable and enjoyable.
My desire for you runs through vessels of my brain through the
heels of my feet.
Covering my whole body with high expectations and sinful
thoughts.

I request, I wish, I hope, I want, I crave
To make a covenant of eternity with you
In my ear and through my eyes . . .
I desire you.

Southern Style

We meet and greet
Polite when we speak
Though the tongue is slurred
If you listen closely you will understand our words
Hospitality is defined by our southern style
We got great history that runs a county mile
In your eyes we may seem slow
Well, thorns and thistles blood sweat and tears shows that we are
always on the go
From hills of corn to turnip greens
From hustling white lighting from whiskey gins
We add flavor in all that we do
From walking for our rights to our lyrical blues
Even though you may not admit who you are on the inside, all the
while
The development of who you are is just grounded from that good
old fashion southern style

Nigga

Darkness, negative, declass, negligence, perplexed, unfaithful, curt, lazy, misleading, thuggish, grimy, evil, demonic, indecisive, ignorant, misunderstood, impolite, argumentative, deceitful, tyrant, captives, belligerent, deceptive, coldhearted, wasteful, unkind, impatient, rebel, lost and merciless.

At some point of time in one's life we either shown ourselves to be that of the name itself through our actions, but note that it never denotes a color of one's attitude.

Why I Cry

I do not hate you for you are always on my mind.

A love this strong I may not ever find

You hold my hand and look into my eyes and tell me that you care.

Well just to let you know inside I feel very scared.

The reason for this is because I have been hurt before, and the fact that you come a long and say that you can love me forever more.

I don't speak, trying to be careful because love is a delicate thing.

Making sure each moment I'm with you I'll remember again and again, so whenever I lay my head back and begin a mournful sigh.

Baby I want you to know these are the reasons why I cry.

Expressions of Endearment

Everything about you truly means something to me.

When you look at me your eyes tell me you are focused and real.

The touch of your hands makes me feel secure as if I know you will always be there to rely upon.

Your hugs are like pillars with strong beams that make me feel wanted.

Your kisses are soft and gentle, that lets me know you have feelings and with each kiss is a expression or message of endearment which makes me want to kiss you forever.

Your words are comforting, knowing you can communicate in a mild spirit. And your smile is part of light to a great path in my life that's filled with sweet sounds, pleasures, desires, fantasies, and surprises.

I love you truly from my creative heart. I long for the day when I am able to express my expressions of endearment thoroughly to you.

I Would Like

I would like to be happy and peaceable with you.

I would like to walk and run hand in hand with you.

I would like to kiss you all over until your body is numb.

I would like to unite with you feeling you inside of me becoming one.

I would like to feel your seed be planted within me.

Just as an alcoholic gets intoxicated from the smell and taste of alcohol I want your tongue and lips to be intoxicated with my chest.

I would like to let you know through my eyes you are the only one I will be committed to.

I would like you to take your time and feel me with heat and watch my skin glisten from sweat by the light of the moon.

I would like you to trace my body with ice and hear the steam in our bedroom.

I would like to be your friend, your lover, your significant other, and your spouse.

I would like to be with you for eternity.

The Bodies of Concinnity

Individually we are rare structures we are incomplete with no meaning or direction.

With your strength and guidance you give me direction.

With my love and understanding I give you meaning.

When our bodies are together, in sync, and as one mentally we help and encourage each other.

When our bodies are together, in sync, and as one emotionally we comfort and understand each other.

When our bodies are together, in sync, and as one emotionally we comfort and understand each other.

When our bodies are together, in sync, and as one physically we feel each other heights of love.

God fully put us together he is with you and I together we are a chorus line of harmony very graceful and elegant we are bodies of concinnity.

Poetic Quotes from the Hearts of Men

The following are poems and quotes from men based on relationships

Love Experience

I've heard, love is something one can't live without
But I have my reason to doubt
How does something so strong just fade away?
And when it does, what then do I say?
I thought love was to last forever
So then, why aren't we still together?
Without love I feel incomplete
And all I have are memories that are more bitter than sweet
Love please don't come knocking at my heart
Cause this time, I'm a little more smart
Bad loving has made me a tougher man
And learning from this Love Experience is my best yet plan
Eric Young

Relationships aren't easy but they can be rewarding. A few essential elements are love, trust, and respect. If you truly love and respect your mate and couple that love with the love of Jehovah this threefold cord will have certain success
Blair Harris

I don't take women for granted. In my culture the woman is always first I look for what's in the heart, I think you can't control the heart
Just knowing that I have someone who can call me and tell me they were thinking about me, it's a feeling that's better than sex
Nesio

We live in a selfish society and for some women it seem that they are not prepared for marriage. The idea of marriage is more of a me attitude. The moral values of marriage have declined it seems people are getting married for the wrong reasons. Values are not engrained in a person like they use to be. Some women are looking for the romantic side of marriage instead of all the realities that come along with like the partnership of a marriage.

Chris

Some of us are products of our environment, for example when it comes to being faithful or unfaithful what we have seen is what we tend to do

Myleek

I have been married for 45 years and from what I see is that men aren't being men they are boys, just want to give up, don't want to take care of their responsibilities and the test that come along with it. I watch so call men and women get married and when the test of time comes around they run, punk out, give up. Everyone wants respect and don't know how to respect themselves first. The thugs and hot pants women of today is not the way a happy relationship starts.

Earl

My Woman

My woman is strong
And can make her own choices
She supports me and doesn't listen to peoples mumble voices
When I'm trippin and talkin crazy
My woman is there to save me
My woman loves her mom and dad
She even loves me when I'm stupid and make her sad
My woman doesn't need me to live on
But has chosen me to be the one she leans on
My woman loves others
More than she loves herself

That's why her Brothers will always be there if she needs help
My woman loves her God
10x more than she loves me
If I went nuts and cheated
She'd be mad but not respond heated
Because their relationship matters more than our companionship
My woman may or may not forgive me
I could be wrong as Adam was
But I'd still need her here with me
But that's not what I'm about
So my woman will never have that reason to shout
Even though I said all that
There's no question where my woman's devotions is at
She may not need me always
But I sure need her when I walk down my darkest hallways
I know what I'm supposed to attain and without her
I'd be overcome by the drain
Swallowed in pools of my own pain
How can I turn guns into roses
If I don't have one with me who's the closest
It'd be like Egypt during the plague of locusts
There'd be no hope
In the which I grope
Without my woman
I don't know if I'd even be human

Trevor

The Colors of Friends

Like colors to an Artist
Black, white, red and shades of blues
Some dark some light
Some closed and some being used
All are needed
Some depleted, still others often mistreated
Wait, stop don't be confused

A true artist knows what colors to choose to paint a picture
So simple so true
A picture so real and truly reflective of you
So be forewarned
Choose carefully dear artist
Before you paint that
Which you'll treasure a lifetime
Because some colors aren't worth a penny, a nickel or a dime
                              Blair Harris

Relationships can be cool when you have two forgiving people
involved and both put forth effort. Because no body wants to fight
alone
                              Keith

You never no what you have until it's gone. I didn't realize I was in
love with this one female until I had already kicked her out
                              Delly Dell

Two people being able to communicate about anything, confiding
in each other; it's about sharing and giving
                              Redbilla

Thank You

I would like to thank the two lives which were combined as one, that produced this living cell.

And the encouragement of friends and family

Thank you for standing beside me behind me and in front of me as shields

Thank you to the ones who had much doubt who spoke of my weaknesses and my faults to you, you are a writer's inspiration

Thank you to the ones who were psychic in telling me how I feel and what I feel without you I wouldn't have had this wall, this wall to climb up and over.

To the boys who allowed me to become a woman in being forgiving to you in words and also through heart. Through our experiences with each other, some of you turned out to be great men. Without those experiences I would not be able to share my story of love and life.

To those who were just plain haters, remember you stand alone, you too are also an inspiration to a writer just the fact of not having a clue of why hatred lingers in you is enough to write a book itself.

And last but not least I would like to thank all those who sold me those wonderful WOOF tickets. Even though they were not redeemable because they didn't back up your actions with them I was able to purchase confidence, self worth, patience, and endurance to continue to try my hardest
But overall, my thank you is based on life's experiences past, present, and future and those that have come into my life and those yet to come into my life.

About The Author

Shu-Wonna Gregory Young is a St. Louis native. Her writing blitz started there while attending Simmons Middle School with an array of Short Stories, essays, and poetry which won her several writing awards from her school and University Chapters.

By late 1991 most of her writings were keyed toward poetry because of the tragic death of her brother in a drunk driving accident, in which "Loosing A Loved One" was composed.

Her writings are based on her life's experiences. Shu-Wonna has been able to share her poetry from performing at local events and spots in Central Illinois and also distribution of poetry to well known businesses.

She is self-made, currently she is working toward a Nursing Degree, more poetry and music.

CPSIA information can be obtained
at www.ICGtesting.com
Printed in the USA
LVOW12s0251070916

503542LV00001B/48/P